T0198752

The True Story

of

Freddie Mercury
THE PARROT

How a Missing Macaw Captured the Hearts of an Entire Community

The True Story of Freddie Mercury The Parrot
HOW A MISSING MACAW CAPTURED THE HEARTS OF AN ENTIRE COMMUNITY

iUniverse books may be ordered through booksellers or by contacting:

iUniverse
1663 Liberty Drive
Bloomington, IN 47403
www.iuniverse.com
844-349-9409

ISBN: 978-1-5320-9278-7 (sc)
ISBN: 978-1-5320-9276-3 (e)
ISBN: 978-1-5320-9277-0 (hc)

Library of Congress Control Number: 2020912305

Print information available on the last page.

iUniverse rev. date: 04/04/2022

The True Story

—— *of* ——

Freddie Mercury
THE PARROT

*How a Missing Macaw Captured the Hearts
of an Entire Community*

VICTOR RASH

Illustrated by Bradley James Geiger

Chapter 1

Everyone Loves a Picnic

On a beautiful summer day a few years ago, several of my friends and I got together for a picnic. We had all been working very hard at our jobs, so we decided that a picnic would be a great way to relax and enjoy being with friends on such a perfect Sunday afternoon. I had no idea that being there that day would change my life forever. While there, I had a chance to spend some time with a good friend named April whom I hadn't seen for quite some time. After we had talked for a while, she began to tell me about her four parrots. That brought back memories of when I, too, had a parrot named Floyd. "I used to have a macaw a long time ago, but I had to give him up," I said. Between working and going to college, I simply didn't have any time to spend with Floyd, which was unfair to him. Parrots are very sociable and enjoy having someone around. It was difficult to let him go. I told April how I had regretted it ever since.

"I know someone who has a bird rescue," April said. "I can give you his phone number, if you would like."

I called Barry, the owner of the rescue, and the very next day I met Freddie for the first time. The rescue was actually located in Barry's house. When I arrived, there were two or three people in the front yard. Just outside the front door of the house was a perch, and sitting on it was the most beautiful parrot I had ever seen. He was a blue-and-gold–scarlet macaw mix, which made him very colorful. His wings had been clipped to keep him from flying away. It didn't take long for me to decide that I wanted him—and the sooner, the better. "It may be a couple of days before I can bring Siren to your house," Barry said. The macaw's name was Siren at the time. He didn't get renamed Freddie until later on.

I wasn't very happy about that, so Barry then gave me an option. "I can bring him to you tomorrow, but it won't be until late in the evening." Barry had just gotten Siren. A vet was coming to check him out the next afternoon, before Barry would let me have him, and Barry had tickets to a baseball game that evening. That was fine with me. So around eleven o'clock the next night, Barry came by with Freddie (Siren), along with the bird's rather large cage. It didn't take long for me to realize how special this macaw was.

Even though Freddie was very young, he appeared to be smart, and he seemed to be different from most parrots that I had been around.

Initially Freddie was named Siren because he made a sound like a siren. I wasn't exactly thrilled with that name, so the very next day I changed it to Freddie Mercury because the bird was so colorful.

Freddie Mercury was the lead singer for the band Queen. It has been said by many that Freddie is the greatest rock and roll singer of all time. He was known for his colorful outfits that he wore onstage while performing. Also, like I said before, something told me that this one-and-a-half-year-old parrot was very special.

As time passed, I began to realize that Freddie was also quite talented. One thing he would do was to take an object normally used to hang his toys with and weave it into a piece of fabric. It would take him about three hours to do this.

Another thing that Freddie was able to do was to make jewelry. One day I hung a toy in his cage for him to play with. He always loved playing with his toys! This one was made up of a chain with several pieces of wood for Freddie to chew up. The chain had a ring on one end and a clip on the other.

The next morning, I found a cool "bracelet" lying in the bottom of his cage. Freddie had attached the clip to the ring to make it look like a bracelet.

He was capable of doing plenty of other interesting things, too. One thing that stood out was the way he removed each and every lock from the nine windows in the Florida room (also known as "Freddie's room"). I then had to secure the screen on the outside to keep Freddie from opening them, too. That room was where he spent most of his time during the day.

But the most remarkable thing that Freddie did was to put on his cape and pretend to be a superhero. He would take one of the pads from the bottom of his cage and drape it over his back. Sometimes he would wear it for a couple of hours while he played with one of his toys.

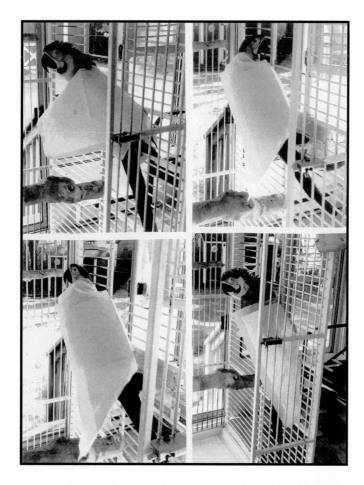

The Florida room was built onto the back of the house many years ago. When Freddie came along, I transformed it into Freddie's room. All of the furniture was removed except for a small sofa that he liked. It was right next to one of the sliding glass doors, so he spent a lot of time on it, especially when it was warm out and the glass door was open. One of his cages was placed out there, along with several perches that I had built using large branches from a sycamore tree.

The room was equipped with its own heating system. During the winter, especially on the days that were bitterly cold, I would turn on the heaters and allow the room to heat up a little before I would let Freddie go out there. After a while, he became more and more anxious to get out there no matter how cold it was. As soon as I would start to unlock the door, he would fly onto my shoulder. I finally gave into him, and from that day on, I allowed Freddie to go out there before the heat was even turned on. On some of those mornings, the temperature was just barely above freezing.

In case you are wondering, Freddie had a second cage, located inside the house. That is where he would sleep during the night. Even though his cage door was always wide open, Freddie would never step foot outside his cage in the morning until he saw me walk out into the living room.

He loved spending time in his room. About the only time that he ever came inside was when I would have a visitor stop by. When he would hear us talking, a lot of times he would come inside to see who it was. He was very sociable. Though Freddie spent most of the day in his room, he was able to enter the main part of the house at any time because I would always leave the door slightly open.

Freddie had really come a long way since the first time I laid eyes on him two and a half years ago. He had definitely worked his way into my heart. I couldn't even begin to imagine how I would feel if anything were ever to happen to him.

Chapter 2

A Time to Play

It was a rather pleasant day for January, considering it was the middle of winter. Freddie had recently celebrated his fourth birthday. The sun was shining brightly, and the temperature that day was expected to reach close to fifty degrees. For the previous several weeks I had been remodeling my basement, and I was finally having the carpet delivered. My friend Joe was scheduled to arrive around midmorning, so I was in the process of preparing for his arrival. My first thought was to feed Freddie and give him some fresh water.

Each and every morning as I fixed his breakfast, Freddie would fly onto my shoulder. That would be the beginning of our morning playtime together. This was a very special time for both of us. He would nip at my ear and neck and play with my hair, and I would grab his beak or one of his feet while he bit at my fingers (in a gentle way, of course). Eventually, I would rub his head as he lowered it onto my shoulder. Freddie absolutely loved for me to do that!

I was just about to go out and fix Freddie's breakfast when I heard Joe's truck pull into the driveway. I was rather anxious to get the carpet off his truck and into the basement, so I decided to put off feeding Freddie until that task was done.

I hurried outside to help Joe but soon realized that I had left my gloves in the house, so I ran inside to get them. I cut through Freddie's room to get back outside, and just as I was taking my first step outside the door, wouldn't you know it, Freddie decided that it was playtime. So Freddie flew onto my shoulder just as I was taking my first step outside. Before I had a chance to realize what was happening, my other foot had reached the second step. Suddenly it hit me that Freddie and I were both outside!

Chapter 3

Up, Up, and Away

So there I was, standing on the second step down from Freddie's room with him on my shoulder. Now what was I going to do?

My immediate reaction was to try to get a hold of him before he had the chance to fly away. So, without any hesitation, I threw my hand back toward him. It was then that Freddie took off straight up into the air!

Even though I had just watched Freddie fly off, I didn't get upset right away. After all, it was a very nice day, even though it was the middle of winter. Along with that, Freddie probably wouldn't wander too far off. But I truly didn't know what to expect, because he had never been outside, except for when I'd first met him, but his wings had been clipped then so that he couldn't fly away.

After we put the carpet in the basement, Joe and I hopped into his truck and began to look around to see where Freddie had gotten to. With all the leaves off the trees, it didn't take long for us to spot him. There he was, in my next-door neighbor's yard, way up in the top of a very tall tree.

Now that I knew where Freddie was, Joe headed off to his next job. As I watched Joe drive away, I began to ponder the situation, but more than anything, I was beginning to blame myself. I felt that if I had handled the situation differently somehow, Freddie wouldn't be way up in that tree all alone. In a couple of days, it was expected to get quite a bit colder. On top of that, I'm sure that he was unaware that there were predators out there that might try to hurt him. I would see hawks flying around this area every day.

There is no doubt that Freddie totally trusted me, so when he flew onto my shoulder and I proceeded to step outside the door, he most likely thought that it was safe out there. And then when I threw my hand back toward him, it probably startled him, causing him to fly off the way he had.

There were a lot of things that I was unsure about at the time, but a couple of things that I was sure about was the fact that, along with the colder temperatures, a winter nor'easter was predicted for Monday or Tuesday (it was presently Thursday afternoon).

One thing that I had going for me was that Freddie was probably getting hungry by now. Remember, I had not had a chance to give Freddie his breakfast. I was hoping and praying that when he got hungry enough, he would come back home. The most important thing for me was to make sure that I knew where Freddie was at all times.

It took less than an hour for him to take flight once again and find out what this newfound freedom was like.

I watched as he flew to the next street over, easily clearing the treetops. After a short flight, he settled in the top of another very tall tree. It was time now for me to get a move on and head over to where he was.

Before I left to go over there, I grabbed one of Freddie's food bowls and filled it with nuts and other food items so that it would make noise when I shook it. As hungry as he must have been by that time, I thought for sure that I could lure him down to me, but after talking to him and shaking his food bowl, and doing whatever else I could think of to get him to fly down to me for over two hours, I started to have doubts. You see, Freddie had a huge appetite, so I really thought my ploy would work. At the house, whenever I called him, he came right to me.

By then, the sun had gone behind the clouds, and it was beginning to feel a bit on the chilly side. Since I hadn't put a coat on when I left to go over there earlier, I decided to run home and get my coat and then return.

Before I started running down the street, I yelled, "Come on, Freddie," a couple of times. Then I took off in the direction of my house. I continued to call Freddie as I was running, but when I looked back, he was still up in the tree. As I approached the end of the street, I looked back again. I wanted to be sure that Freddie could see what direction I was going in. As I turned my head to look back one more time, before I made the turn at the end of the street, I saw that Freddie was flying out of the tree and heading toward me. I was very excited that something good was finally starting to happen!

Freddie caught up to me as I was making the first turn. Right around the second turn was where my house was located. Phew! We were almost home! However, as I made my way around that final turn, I looked back just in time to watch Freddie settle on the branch of a tree no more than one hundred feet from my driveway. A couple of neighbors and I tried to talk him into coming down. It became obvious that Freddie wasn't going to budge. I felt better knowing that he was close by, but the thought that he would have to remain out in the cold all by himself with no food and no water was very upsetting for me. It was very sad that he was out there alone, and along with him being cold, there was no doubt in my mind that he was also very hungry and thirsty. I didn't know if Freddie was going to be able to get any sleep that night. As for me, it was unlikely that I would get any at all.

By then the sun was going down. It would be dark soon. My neighbor's patio was almost right below the tree Freddie was in, so we decided to put one of his perches out there with some food on it. My neighbor Gina put the patio light on and kept an eye out the entire evening, but Freddie never came down.

I got up the next morning after the sun had risen. I may have dozed off for a short time, but that was about all the sleep I was able to get. I got dressed as quickly as I could so that I could go check on Freddie. When I got there, he was gone. He hadn't touched any of the food that I'd put out for him.

I jumped in my car and rode through the neighborhood, hoping that I would spot Freddie up in a tree somewhere. Then I could continue my effort to capture him. I prayed that I would get him back home before something bad happened to him.

As I was cruising around, I received a phone call from my neighbor Linda. I explained what had happened. Right away she said, "Put it on Facebook to get the word out." That way, if anyone happened to spot Freddie, they could simply let me know where he was. That was an awesome idea because now there would be eyes everywhere looking for him.

Quite a bit of time had passed when finally I got a call from a woman who had seen the story on the internet. She said she was getting in her car when she heard some loud squawking coming from a nearby tree. When she looked up, it wasn't hard to spot the brightly colored parrot sitting on a branch at the top of the tree in her backyard.

Chapter 4

I'll Be Back

When I got the address where Freddie had been spotted, I headed over there as fast as I could. As I got close to the location given to me, I noticed three people standing out in the street and looking into a tree. I was sure this was the right place. Freddie had flown about two miles to get there.

I parked the car and headed over to where everyone was standing. Freddie knew that it was me. Right away he started squawking really loud and moving side to side as if he were excited to see me.

I began telling everyone how Freddie had gotten out. Then one of them asked me, "How do you plan on catching him?"

Not having a truly solid answer, I said, "For the time being, I am merely keeping tabs on his location and doing whatever I can to coax him down to me." I knew that by now Freddie must be really hungry. So, for lack of knowing what else I could do, I continued to talk to him as I rattled his food bowl.

I had gotten there around the middle of the afternoon. Now it was after five o'clock, and I still hadn't had any success. It was getting dark as the sun continued to go down, and I was beginning to feel a chill in the air. The neighbors who had stayed with me for those couple of hours were now heading back to their homes.

There wasn't much else I could do at the time, so I hollered, "Goodbye—I'll be back," as I walked toward my car. Whenever I would leave the house to go somewhere, I would always say to Freddie, "Goodbye—I'll be back," and he would repeat it back to me as I was walking to the door. But this time Freddie didn't respond. Perhaps the cold, along with not having had anything to eat or drink for two days, was starting to affect him.

It was very difficult to get in my car and drive away, leaving Freddie way up in that tree. The temperature was beginning to drop, and the wind was starting to blow a little bit harder. It would get dark a little bit after five o'clock, and I would go to work at six but get done around ten thirty. After I got done working that Friday night, I ate dinner alone. Freddie and I would usually eat dinner at about the same time. I would feed him while my dinner was cooking. Then, when I went into the living room to eat, he would fly over to my chair to see what I had. About the only thing that I didn't share with him was chicken (for obvious reasons). I sure did miss Freddie. I went to bed a lot earlier than usual. I wanted to make sure that I was alert and ready for whatever I had to face the next day.

I awoke to the sound of my next-door neighbors Skip and Linda talking loudly in their backyard. About that time the phone rang. It was Skip, telling me that Freddie was in his yard, way up in a tree. I hurried over there to see. There was Freddie, in the same tree that he had flown to when he'd first gotten out two days ago. That sure did lift my spirits. It gave me hope that I was going to get him back!

I was starting to think that, along with all his other skills, Freddie possessed a rather keen sense of direction. After all, when I'd left him the night before, he was two miles away! And don't forget that he had never been outside before, so it wasn't as if he was familiar with the territory.

Skip, Linda, and I tried for quite a while to get him to come down. Once again, I even put one of Freddie's perches in my backyard with a bunch of food on it. However, for some unknown reason, he just wouldn't come down. Although this tactic hadn't worked the night before when I put the perch on my neighbor's patio, now it was in a place that Freddie was familiar with: his own backyard. I couldn't understand why he wouldn't come to me.

After a while, Freddie once again took flight and headed for the next street over. This time he went in the opposite direction of the street to which he had traveled on the first day that he got out.

So off I went again in an attempt to capture him somehow and get him back home where he belonged. Neighbors would come out to see if I was having any luck. "Is there anything we can do to help?" they offered. Sadly, there wasn't really anything anyone could do. But although there wasn't anything the neighbors could do to help me catch Freddie, the fact that they'd offered helped me in a different way: they made me feel like I wasn't alone.

After doing what I had been doing for close to three hours, I began to get really frustrated. I had been calling to Freddie while continuing to rattle his food bowl, and I'd run down the street several times while calling his name. I was hoping he would follow me like he had before. I even started to get mad at Freddie for not coming to me after all this time. "Stay up there if that's what you want to do!" I yelled. About that time, it started to rain a little bit. I stuck around for a while, thinking that the rain would help to entice him to come down. But after another twenty minutes or so, I finally said to Freddie, "Fine, if you want to stay up there, then stay up there, but I'm going home!" In reality, although I may have thought that I was mad at Freddie, I was mad at myself for having let this happen and then for being upset that I couldn't help my bird.

I had been home for just a little while when the phone rang. It was a woman calling from California. After talking to her for a few minutes, I discovered she seemed to know quite a lot about the situation that I was in. She had become aware of Freddie's being out through social media. I went on to tell her about the way I had gotten mad and gone home, leaving Freddie out in the rain. When I told her that, she got pretty upset with me. She went on to explain that Freddie wanted to come down to me, but he simply didn't know how. That made me feel awful, because just a few minutes ago I had gotten mad at him for not coming down.

"He flies all around the house every day," I said.

In response to that, she said, "Flying in the house is completely different from flying way up like Freddie has been doing." To give me some perspective, she explained, "It's like learning to ride a bicycle." I guess she meant that it can be scary when learning to ride a bike because if you mess up, you can get hurt.

That made sense to me. On at least one occasion when I kept calling to him, Freddie would leave the tree that he was in and fly around in a circle while looking down. Eventually, he would just land in another tree. He probably was trying to get to me but couldn't figure out how to do it.

The California woman told me another very interesting fact. She made me aware that once Freddie settled in a tree for the night, he would remain there until the following morning. Once the sun rises, birds generally fly off in search of food and water. She had come to learn these things through her work with eagles and other wild birds.

She told me one more thing before we ended our conversation: that the amount of flying Freddie was doing was using up all of the energy he otherwise needed to conserve in order to stay warm during the cold winter nights. That really worried me because he was doing a lot of flying. And because he was staying so high up in the trees, he wasn't getting any food.

"Thank you so much for your help," I said. As soon as I finished talking to her, I hurried back over to where Freddie was. It was just beginning to get dark around that time. When I got there, he was gone.

Chapter 5

The Storm Is upon Us

It was now late in the afternoon on Saturday. It had become completely dark, and all I could think about was Freddie being out there all by himself.

The weather continued to be in my favor. It would still get pretty cold at night, though. On that particular evening, the temperature was expected to get down to about thirty-five degrees. I remembered the mornings when Freddie would go out to his room with the temperature being even lower than that. I was hoping that those prior experiences would somehow help him to cope with the colder temperatures that he was contending with now. Macaws are native to Mexico, Central America, and South America. The climates there are warm, and there are rain forests. The trees provide nuts, berries, seeds, and much cover from predators.

It was just about time for me to go to work, so I had to hurry up and get ready. That was the last thing I felt like doing. There wasn't really anything else I could do about Freddie until the next morning, so off I went. I figured that going to work would help take my mind off Freddie, but in reality that didn't happen.

When I woke up on Sunday morning, I was quite anxious to start looking for Freddie again. For some reason, I had a feeling that he was somewhere close by. I drove down to the end of the street. I wasn't sure which way I was going to go. As I looked to the left, I couldn't believe what I saw! Two people were standing together a short distance away, and one of them was pointing into a tree. Sure enough, it was Freddie perched high up in a tree behind the house.

By this time, Freddie was into his fourth day away from home. Because I hadn't had a chance to feed him on the day that he got out, he was also entering his fourth day with nothing to eat. I'd like to think that he was at least able to get some sleep, but considering the conditions, any sleep he may have gotten probably didn't amount to much.

During the entire span of six or seven hours that I spent there with Freddie that day, with the exception of two short breaks at the house, he never left that spot. That was probably a good thing because with no food and very little sleep, he really needed to conserve his energy. At this point in time, I began to realize that he wasn't going to fly down to me. I was mainly there just to keep him from being alone.

The day was coming to an end. As the sun was going down, I bid farewell to Freddie once more and headed back home. Leaving him up in that tree, knowing how tired and hungry he must have been, was one of the most difficult things I've ever done. Each night when I left to go home, I would always say, "Goodbye! I'll be back!" I was happy knowing where Freddie was. I could go back there in the morning before the sun came up, and he would still be there.

As comforting as that thought was, there was something else that was making me a nervous wreck. The winter nor'easter was still heading our way and was expected to hit us within the next twenty-four hours. Wind speeds were predicted to reach seventy miles per hour and possibly even higher in some places.

After breakfast I loaded the car up with essentials—food and water for both Freddie and me—and headed back over to where he was. I could see his silhouette against the sky as the sun began to rise. I hollered to him to let him know I was there. *"Squawk! Squawk!"* Freddie responded.

As the sun rose, I could feel the temperature rising from the near-freezing temperatures of the night before. It was shaping up to be a pretty nice day. However, this was not going to last. Just a few hours away was that nor'easter, heading right for us. Freddie remained in the same spot he had been in since the previous afternoon. Knowing he hadn't been exerting a lot of energy was a good thing. However, this also meant that he most likely hadn't had anything to eat or drink in that length of time. I couldn't help but think that before long, Freddie was going to be on the move again.

And sure enough, it wasn't long before Freddie once again took flight. Incredibly, he was actually heading in the direction of his home, which was only a couple of blocks away. I quickly followed him as he made the turn and headed up the street. He was way ahead of me, so I ran back to my car and raced to catch up to him.

What a relief! As I rode toward my house in search of where Freddie may have landed, I soon spotted him in a tree directly across the street from his home.

A short time later, my friend Gary showed up. I asked him if he would help me move Freddie's cage to the backyard, where Freddie would be able to see it from his location in the tree. It all seemed so simple. There is no doubt that Freddie was extremely hungry. I felt that it was just a matter of time before he would fly down to his cage, where he knew there would be something to eat.

By then it was well into the afternoon. I was convinced now that Freddie really did not know how to fly downward.

As the afternoon went on, it became cloudier and the wind began to pick up. It was then that Freddie decided to fly off. Perhaps he was hoping it would be nicer elsewhere. I was heartbroken. With the storm inching its way into our area, it was looking fairly unlikely that I was going to be able to get Freddie in before the nor'easter reached full force.

Once again, I located Freddie in a tree not far away. However, time was running out. The wind was blowing a lot harder now, and the sky was much darker as the clouds increased. Sunset was coming. Soon the darkness would be complete.

I kept my eyes on Freddie as he slowly disappeared into the blackness. All I could do now was pray to God that He would protect Freddie and enable him to survive this dangerous storm that was upon us.

Chapter 6

Where's Freddie?

That Monday night was absolutely the worst night that I have ever had to endure in my entire life. It was unlikely that Freddie would be able to remain in the tree that he'd been perched in when the sun went down. That tree was so thinned out that there was no way it could provide any protection at all for Freddie. Every thought that entered my mind that night was a bad one. My macaw had to be terrified. I kept thinking about what he was up against—and with nothing to eat or drink for such a long time. Would he have enough strength to survive? It got to me so much that I broke into tears many times that night.

When it was almost time for the sun to come up, I headed over to where Freddie had been the night before. Just as I expected, he was gone.

It had been raining hard with the wind blowing at sixty miles per hour. The rain was practically coming down sideways. I began to ride around the neighborhood to see if I could spot Freddie. After a while, seeing that he was nowhere in sight, I finally decided to head back home. I was hoping Freddie would take refuge in a pine tree; he most likely wouldn't stay in a tree with no leaves, because it wouldn't offer him any protection. Then the thought came to me: if Freddie were in a thick pine tree, I wouldn't be able to see him. All I could do was wait it out.

The entire day went by without my receiving even one call from anyone saying they had seen Freddie. As daytime turned into nighttime, the rain began to slow up, and the wind speed decreased quite a bit. It was still a miserable night, but at least the conditions were improving.

I was in for another very long night. All I could think about was whether or not Freddie would be able to survive the horrible storm. I prayed a lot that night, asking God to keep Freddie safe. This was the first day that had gone by in which no one had seen him. As bad as it was, I never gave up hope that I would find him out there somewhere.

It seemed to take forever for morning to finally arrive so that I could begin the search for my beloved Freddie. More people, some whom I hardly knew, offered to help. It was amazing how many people were out looking for him. Even a mailman named Bob, who also had a parrot, took a half day off from work to help in the search. By the middle of the afternoon, with no sightings of Freddie anywhere, I began to wonder if he perhaps hadn't survived the storm. It also crossed my mind that he could be lying somewhere with some sort of injury.

As the day went on, I continued to hope and pray that he was okay. My faith was strong, but I really needed to hear something positive. Sometimes people say that no news is good news, but that certainly was not the case here. There was no doubt in my mind that there were a lot of people out there looking for my bird. As deeply as everyone had become involved with this story over the last several days, there was no way that anyone would be able to walk away from it.

Finally, around four o'clock, my prayers were answered. Someone named Stacy sent me a voice mail informing me that an individual had posted on Facebook that Freddie was in a tree at a location approximately two miles from my house. The young woman who had posted on Facebook probably didn't know how to contact me directly, so when Stacy saw the message on Facebook, she called me to tell me where Freddie was located.

I was riding around looking for Freddie when I got the message, so it didn't take long for me to arrive at the house where he was. I was greeted in the driveway by Jennifer, who was the one who had posted on Facebook, and her young daughter. They wasted no time pointing at Freddie, who was sitting way up in a tree behind their house. Jennifer suggested that I could probably get closer to him if I drove around to the street behind her house. To this day, I still don't know how he survived that storm.

When I drove to the next street over, it put me directly below the tree Freddie was in. I was very happy and relieved to see him again. From what I could tell, he appeared to be okay.

As thrilled as I was that Freddie had survived that terrible storm the day before, I still didn't know how I was going to capture him. It wasn't going to be getting dark for a while. When the sun finally started to go down, I could feel the cold setting in. I didn't have a coat to wear. Nevertheless, I had to stay there until it was completely dark to ensure that I would know where to find Freddie the next morning. During the hour or so that I was there, about all I did was talk to Freddie and be there with him in the hope that it would comfort him.

I was there alone for a while. Then I saw someone walking toward me. When he got to where I was, he said, "Hi. I'm Fran, Jennifer's husband. We thought that you might be chilly, so I brought you this coat to wear. Jennifer made you this cup of hot chocolate." What a nice gesture that was. Fran stayed with me until it was completely dark. I hated to leave Freddie every night when the sun went down, but until I could come up with a better idea, that was all I could do.

Chapter 7

No Rest for the Weary

Freddie had been gone for a week now. I must say, frustration was starting to set in. I was spending each and every day, from sunrise to sunset, trying to coax him into flying down to me, with no success. I was starting to wonder if Freddie ever would come down. I went to work at 6:00 every night, except for Thursday and Sunday. I worked until 10:30 p.m. Luckily for me, I only work at night, so I was able to devote the days to Freddie.

I had loaded up the car the night before. Once again, I headed over to where I had previously left Freddie. When I arrived, I parked the car, got my chair from the trunk, and placed it at the side of the road. As the sun continued to rise, I could soon see Freddie. It was then that he let out a couple of loud squawks. He knew that I had come back to be with him.

I had been sitting for about half an hour when a police car pulled up. The officer walked over to a nearby house and began talking with someone there. Whoever lived there must have called the police to find out why someone was sitting in a chair nearby and looking up into a tree. A short time later, the police officer proceeded to where I was sitting. He pointed to my car. "Are you the owner of that car?" he asked.

"Yes I am, sir," I replied.

"May I see your driver's license, please?" the officer asked. I handed him the license.

"I suppose you're wondering what I'm doing here?" I asked. I pointed to Freddie. "That's my parrot up in that tree," I explained. "I'm merely trying to get him to come down to me."

The officer walked back to the same house. After a short conversation, he came back over to me. "Thank you for your cooperation," he said. As he was walking back to his patrol car, he turned around. "Good luck catching him!" he called.

When I had arrived around seven o'clock, a light rain was falling. Now the sky was getting brighter as the clouds were breaking up. It was turning out to be a pretty nice day. That was all well and good, but for it to be a *truly nice day*, I needed to get Freddie back.

I glanced at my watch. It was just after ten o'clock. Darkness did not fall until around five o'clock in winter in my area. I was going to be in for a really long day.

Suddenly, my cell phone rang. The call was from a woman who had learned of Freddie's predicament on social media. It was comforting just to talk about what was happening, even though I did not even know the caller. When I found out who she was and what help she had to offer, it made me feel very happy and excited; you have no idea.

"My husband, Ron, owns a tree trimming company," the caller explained. "He is willing to bring his truck, equipped with a boom that can lift a person as high as a hundred feet, to reach Freddie. He would also bring some of his crew to assist."

"I needed for something to happen to lift my spirits, and this is just the thing!" I answered.

It was going to be at least an hour until the truck from the tree service arrived. While I was waiting for the truck to show up, another type of vehicle caught my eye as it pulled over to the side of the road and stopped. It certainly wasn't difficult to recognize it. It was the WDEL news van. WDEL is the largest news and talk radio station in the area. An individual soon exited the vehicle and began walking toward me.

I would soon find out that it was Amy Cherry, the assistant news director at the radio station. After I introduced myself to her, I said, "What brings you out here?"

Amy replied, "There's a website that I visit now and then, and in recent days, the main topic of conversation has been about the parrot that has gotten loose. I decided to come check it out."

She then asked me for an interview. I said, "Of course." I began by telling her how Freddie had gotten out and how helpless I was in trying to capture him given the fact that he had consistently been hanging out in the very tops of the tallest trees. I went on to tell her what the woman from California had told me. "He wants to come down to me, but he simply doesn't know how." Right after I had told her all of that about Freddie being so high up, as if from a movie script, here came Ron and his crew from Ron's Tree Service. I told Amy about the conversation I had had with Ron's wife earlier and added that the guys from the tree service were here to help.

Meanwhile, Ron positioned his truck to a spot where he could reach Freddie. For insurance reasons I was not allowed up in the bucket. I went along with the plan even though I didn't think that Freddie would allow a stranger to get that close to him. One of the guys from Ron's crew would have to attempt the rescue. All I could do was watch and pray that this effort would have a successful outcome.

Chapter 8

Catch Me if You Can

As soon as this stranger got close to him, Freddie took off. Fortunately, he did not fly far. I could not help but think that to have the best chance of catching him, I would have to be the one to go up in the bucket. Ron agreed to let me give it a try.

After securing me in the harness and completing other safety measures, Ron began raising me up to my beloved Freddie. I had not been close to Freddie for a whole week. Ron did a great job placing me within an arm's length of my elusive bird. The bucket held steady, but with the wind blowing the tree branches back and forth, my task was not going to be easy.

As I continued talking to Freddie, I waited for the right time to take a chance at grabbing hold of him. A small branch got between us, just enough to keep me from getting a grip. Freddie flew off—again. This time he landed in the closest tree, just a short fifty yards away. These short flights he was taking made me believe that perhaps he was just plain tired.

I was pretty upset that I had gotten so close to Freddie and yet was unable to get a hold of him. Little did I know that something even more upsetting was about to happen. As I stood there at eye level with Freddie, suddenly a large hawk flew into the same tree. A hawk—alarmingly close to Freddie!

I was freaking out, not knowing what the outcome of this dangerous encounter was going to be. Worst of all, there was not a thing I could do to prevent it. In seconds, the hawk and Freddie started fighting. They locked onto each other, flapping their wings. This went on for several long seconds. By now my heart was beating out of my chest! Freddie had to be tired, and he was most likely weak from not eating all week. After a short fight, I guess the hawk decided he didn't want anything to do with Freddie. The hawk flew away in defeat. You have no idea how relieved I was. When I first met Freddie, I felt that he was special. Now I was starting to think that he was also quite amazing.

Remember in the beginning of this story how I told of how talented Freddie is? Now there was yet another accomplishment—scaring off hawks. The coolest thing of all was that Amy Cherry from WDEL had captured the entire incident on video.

With all the excitement, Freddie and I were beginning to attract quite a bit of attention. Along with Amy, Ron and his crew, and me, there were now a dozen neighbors following us around. It was afternoon now. We were all getting hungry, so I ordered pizza and drinks for everyone, even the neighbors taking part in the journey.

After everyone had eaten, Ron got right back to doing what he had come for. He was extremely focused on this difficult task. After several more failed attempts, we decided it was time to call it a day. Amy gathered her equipment, as did Ron. As he was leaving, he called, "I'll be back in the morning." I was so grateful for all he had done that I wanted to pay him, but he wouldn't take a cent. As you will soon see, he was far from being done.

I stayed there for a while, waiting for dark, when Freddie would settle in for the night. As I was standing there, another reporter from WDEL walked up to me. "Would you mind if I interview you before you leave?" he asked.

"Of course not," I told him. As we began talking about the events of the day and what I planned to do next, it suddenly hit me: *I may never get Freddie back.*

With that awful thought in mind, about halfway into the interview, I began crying my eyes out. The interviewer gave me a hug, trying to comfort me. "Everything is going to turn out just fine," he said.

I could only hope and pray that he was right.

Chapter 9

Help Is on the Way

As Friday morning rolled around, I couldn't believe that Freddie was beginning his eighth day on the loose. Ron showed up around eight o'clock, just as he had promised. He was eager to get started, and this time he had a rather large fishing net. The hope was that the net would allow him to reach out for Freddie without getting too close.

We never had a chance to find out if the net idea would work. As soon as Ron raised the bucket, Freddie flew away. This time, instead of going just a short distance, he cleared the treetops. We watched as he continued to fly completely out of sight. That was actually not such a bad thing, though. Freddie was headed in the direction of home.

Sure enough, I found him in the wooded area at the school near our house. It was almost the exact area he had been found in a few days earlier. I was encouraged. It seemed that Freddie knew his way around the area. I stayed with him there until well into the afternoon, when my cell phone rang. The call was from Amy Cherry from WDEL. She had made arrangements with experts from the Three Palms Zoo in lower Delaware. Once before she had used them to help capture a bird, and they were successful. Now they were on their way here to help capture Freddie.

In the meantime, the plan was to locate Freddie and then, when darkness came, work along with Ron's Tree Service. As the experts reminded me, it was likely that Freddie would be settled down for the night. Luck should then be on their side since macaws do not see well in complete darkness. With the use of a net on a very long pole, the capture would hopefully be guaranteed.

Freddie was still located in the middle of the thick group of trees at the nearby school. This was a problem. We needed to get Freddie to a location where Ron would be able to get close with the boom and bucket. "Perhaps I can get Freddie to follow me as he did once before," I said.

As I had done earlier, I began running toward our house while hollering Freddie's name. As he had done previously, he started to follow me. He caught up to me quickly and flew past me. Amazingly, when Freddie reached the corner, he took a right and flew up our street. I was very happy that something positive was happening.

The happiness was short-lived, though. Suddenly Freddie began flying really fast in the opposite direction. A hawk was chasing him back toward the school. The chase continued until both birds were out of sight. We needed to locate Freddie soon. The workers from the zoo would be arriving at dusk. With no Freddie, it would be a wasted trip for them.

It was getting close to five o'clock now, just beginning to get dark. Freddie was nowhere to be found. There were dozens of people out looking for him. I knew that for a fact. Time was running out. Suddenly my phone rang. It was Amy Cherry, calling to tell me that Freddie had been located in a development about three miles away. When I asked her who had found him, she replied, "It was the guys from the zoo." With so many people out looking, I thought it very interesting that they would be the ones to find Freddie. I have no idea what led them to him.

I was already driving around in my car, so I got to Freddie quickly. Before long, the WDEL news van and Ron's Tree Service arrived. Ron and the zoo workers began planning how they would attempt the rescue. Ron looked around for a place to position his truck. Once that was decided on, the zoo workers secured themselves in the bucket. Then Ron raised them upward very slowly to avoid scaring Freddie.

From the ground, we couldn't see exactly what was happening. We could see some movement up there as we watched in silence. Then the silence was broken by the sound of Freddie's wings flapping as he flew off.

It was pretty dark that night and hard to see what direction Freddie had flown in. Neighbors had joined the workers in keeping watch over what was going on. With so many eyes looking upward, I felt that someone was bound to spot him.

"There he is," a woman shouted, pointing a finger to the sky. Sure enough, there was Freddie, his bright orange chest standing out against the blackness.

We watched as Freddie flew into a tree in a neighboring backyard. That was a problem because the yard had a fence around it. Now we needed to figure out a way to cause Freddie to fly to a tree outside the yard so Ron could reach him with the boom.

One of Ron's guys was holding a ball about the size of a tennis ball. "Freddie is way too high for anyone to be able to throw the ball anywhere near him," I said.

"I think I can reach him with the ball, but not by throwing it," Ron's helper replied.

I watched as he placed the ball in a pouch attached to a long cord and began spinning the ball in a circle. When the ball was spinning fast enough, the worker released it. We all stood watching as it whizzed upward through the branches of the tree where Freddie was sitting, although the ball did not come close enough on this first try.

Confident that he could be successful on a second try, the man took aim and set the ball to spinning again. Then he let it go. We could all hear as the ball continued upward, hitting branches along the way. Suddenly Freddie took off. "It worked!" I shouted as Freddie landed in another tree. Thankfully this tree was in a spot where Ron's boom could reach him.

I suggested we take a break in order to give Freddie some time to calm down. Then I wished the zoo experts luck as Ron raised them to the new resting spot. As they reached the needed height, they took great care, hoping Freddie would not become frightened again. Then they made their move. We could see the net at the end of the long pole being guided toward the tree where Freddie was resting. Everyone on the ground was very quiet as we listened to the soft rustling of branches. By now there were at least two dozen residents of the neighborhood who had joined us in this quest to capture Freddie!

The next sound we heard, to our dismay, was the flapping of Freddie's wings as he flew away. Once again, he landed behind a house. It was well after nine o'clock now, and the workers from the downstate zoo had a long drive ahead of them. Sadly, I sent them on their way.

"Thank you both ever so much for making the trip up here and for the great effort you put forth," I told them. I thanked Ron's Tree Service again as well, and then I turned toward home.

There had been so many disappointments, and I was running out of ideas. All I could think of was Freddie out there in the cold of winter. Before I went to bed, I said my prayers as always. I wouldn't be wrong if I were to say I prayed harder that night than ever before. My plea was that something, somehow, would happen that would help me get Freddie back.

Chapter 10

Police on the Scene

It was after nine o'clock when I woke up the next morning. While I was fixing my breakfast, the phone rang. It was my friend Chip, who lives in the neighborhood where I had left Freddie last night. "I saw Freddie flying around earlier, but I haven't seen him since," Chip told me.

"I'll be over as soon as I'm done with breakfast," I said. I was soon on my way. Hopefully, Chip would be able to point out the direction in which Freddie had flown.

"He was circling at the time, so it's hard to say which way he ended up going," Chip explained.

As usual, I began driving around to see if I could spot Freddie up in a tree somewhere. Earlier in the week, WDEL had created a program segment called "Freddie Watch" to keep people informed of all that was going on in the rescue of this elusive parrot.

As I continued to drive around, I couldn't believe what I was seeing. In practically every vehicle I passed, there was someone looking up into the trees. Obviously, they were helping to find Freddie. This went on the entire day, but Freddie was nowhere to be found.

Around 5:30 p.m. I received a report of a sighting only a couple of blocks from my house. When I went to check it out, I was pleasantly surprised to see Ron from Ron's Tree Service on the scene. Ron had also been informed of the sighting. We searched the area, but still Freddie was nowhere to be found. It was dark now, and I had to be at work at six o'clock.

"Thanks, Ron, for being there for me again," I said. Then I rushed home to get ready for work.

When I got to my job, I found it very hard to concentrate. My mind was very focused on Freddie. All I could think about was where he might be and what may have happened to him.

About an hour and a half into my shift at work, I received a phone call from Amy Cherry. My prayers had been answered once again!

A police department across the Delaware–Pennsylvania state line had received information about Freddie. A parrot had been spotted on the roof of a house in the area of West Chester, Pennsylvania. Officer Wassell of the Westtown–East Goshen Police Department had arrived on the scene around 3:30 in the afternoon. He'd taken a picture of the bird on the roof and posted it online. Then a WDEL listener had seen the picture and contacted the radio station.

For the last ten days since Freddie got out, he had been spending all his time in the tops of trees, which made it very hard to capture him. Now he had come down to where it would be much easier for me to catch him. In my heart I somehow had known that if I prayed hard enough, something like this would happen.

Now Amy Cherry was sending the picture to me on my phone. "Is this Freddie?" Amy's text asked.

"Yes!" I replied. "Where is he?"

"He's up in the West Chester area, a few miles past the state line," Amy said.

I was astonished. The West Chester area was a good ten miles from the house in Delaware where Freddie had been seen just that morning. "Is Freddie still there?" I asked.

Amy's reply was all too familiar. "Well, he was until the ladder truck from the West Chester Fire Department arrived. That's when Freddie took off." The Westtown–East Goshen police had called in the fire department.

I needed to know what direction Freddie had taken when he flew from the roof. Was he finally down closer to the ground? I hoped so. That would show he was tired and pretty much done with flying. Likely he was hungry too, and therefore unable to go on like this much longer. "I'll contact one of the officers on the scene when Freddie flies," Amy promised.

The officer got in touch with me just a little later, and we arranged a meeting place. I called Fran, who had kindly given me hot cocoa and an extra warm jacket when I was searching in his neighborhood for Freddie. "Would you be willing to go with me up to West Chester to help find Freddie?" I asked. He agreed to go along. Fran was very active in the search to locate Freddie ever since that night I'd met him, and to be honest, I didn't want to go there by myself. I thought I could really use the company.

We were soon on our way to meet the policeman waiting in his patrol car. We quickly arrived at the meeting place. "I'm Officer Diamond from the Westtown–East Goshen police," he said, introducing himself. We followed him as we headed out in the direction where he had seen Freddie.

The short drive led us to a row of pine trees close to the house where Freddie had flown from the roof. "He has to be right along here somewhere," I said. If I was wrong, we were all just wasting our time.

Officer Diamond, Fran, and I spread out along the row of pine trees. The trees formed a border along the back of the property and were thick with branches. It was difficult to see through them, even with the flashlights we had. We searched and searched for a good hour and a half. I was starting to wonder how much longer Officer Diamond was going to be able to stay and help us.

"I found him!" Officer Diamond announced. What a relief it was to hear those words. I ran over to him and looked up in the tree where he was shining his flashlight. There was Freddie, sitting on a branch about twenty feet up.

The homeowners must have been watching all along, as they soon joined us in the yard. "Freddie is sure to stay in that tree until sunrise," I assured. "That is the habit of parrots." I could return the next morning and try to get him to come down to me with no one else around to distract him.

I then asked if I might have permission to return just before sunrise to try to capture Freddie. The owners were fine with that and even offered to have a light on so I could see. The stage was set. In just a few hours I would find out if I would succeed at what no one had been able to do in nine long days. Gratefully I thanked those who so recently had helped me and was then on my way home. Home. Would Freddie be joining me on the next ride there?

Chapter 11

Putting the Plan into Action

Well before dawn on Sunday, I climbed into my car and set out for the rescue. The sky was still dark. That was important because I did not want to be late and find that Freddie had moved.

Happily I arrived in plenty of time to get everything ready. I had loaded the car the night before with what I considered to be the essentials: my chair, a large fishnet, a towel, a blanket, and bits of the food that Freddie loved to eat. I placed the chair under Freddie's tree, put the net beside it (covered by the blanket so Freddie would not see it), and then scattered the bits of food on the ground. Now there was nothing to do but wait for the sun to come up.

Soon the sun began to rise. It was a clear day, so the sky brightened up quickly. As I kept an eye on Freddie, I could see he was starting to move around. Hoping to lure him down to me, I began talking to him. Calmly and softly I kept it up. It did not take long for him to decide to take flight. However, instead of flying down toward me, he chose to fly back over to the roof of the house.

I quickly grabbed a Nutter Butter cookie, Freddie's most favorite treat. Leaving the net and everything else behind, I headed over to the house. I could see the wife standing just inside the back door, right below where Freddie was sitting on the roof. "Please," I begged, "stay inside until I have this chance to catch him."

Freddie had moved closer to me, right to the edge of the roof. I tried to give him the cookie but could not reach that high. It was then that he flew down to a large round bush just below. There was Freddie, sitting only a couple of feet away. My emotions were running wild, but I couldn't let that affect what I was about to do. Failure was not an option. I continued talking to him as I handed him the cookie. As he was taking it from me, I grabbed him! Now my emotions were at their peak! There were tears of joy at first. Then a big smile came to my face as I began to realize that I had finally gotten Freddie back!

The homeowners had been watching all the while inside their door. As soon as they saw me grab Freddie, they came outside to congratulate me. Together we walked Freddie to the car. It was cold that morning, so I started the car and let it warm up for the ride home. Freddie seemed quite happy tucked under my arm.

The car had been running awhile now, so I placed Freddie inside, gave my thanks to the homeowners, and got into the driver's seat. Freddie had made himself comfortable on the headrest of the passenger seat. Just as I began backing out, a police cruiser made its way up the driveway. It was Officer Wassell, who had taken the picture of Freddie on the rooftop. His arrival gave me the opportunity to thank him for making this glorious day possible.

"If it weren't for you, I would not be here with this big smile on my face," I told him. We had a picture taken together, and then Freddie and I were on our way home!

We were barely on the road when my phone rang. It was Ron wanting to know if I needed help in any way. He had told me earlier that he and one of his crew would be nearby in case I needed him. What a great guy. "We left the residence a minute ago, and right now Freddie and I are on our way home," I told him.

"Have you told Amy yet?" Ron asked.

"I haven't had a chance to call anybody yet," I told him. He promised to tell her the good news. I talked to Freddie only a little bit during the ride home. I just kept thinking about how happy everyone was going to be when they heard the good news.

When I pulled into my driveway, I saw my next-door neighbors Skip and Linda all dressed up for church. They must have seen Freddie because they came right over. Linda happily took Freddie's picture and immediately put it on Facebook with the news that he had been caught.

Word of Freddie's rescue was spreading fast. I turned on my TV, and there on the Sunday morning news was the picture of Freddie that Linda had just taken. I could hardly believe my eyes and ears. News reporters were telling about Freddie's capture, when it had taken place only an hour ago.

Freddie was not impressed. All he wanted to do was to settle down for a good sleep. After eating his breakfast, he went right to the cage he usually slept in at night. This was not his normal routine. As far back as I could remember, Freddie's habit was to go right to his room and his toys during daylight hours. Just as he was dozing off, the crew from a TV station stopped by to videotape him and to interview me on how he had been captured. Freddie was a real trouper as he climbed out of his cage to greet the crew. Meanwhile, some neighbors, along with some people who had helped with the search, appeared.

Soon the house was quiet again, so Freddie made his way back to his perch to get some much-needed sleep. It wasn't long before two more visitors made their way to the front door. There was no way that I could refuse them. It was Amy Cherry and her husband, who is a photographer for WDEL. After all Amy had done to help get Freddie back, she was finally going to meet him up close.

I led Amy to Freddie's cage in the dining room. Even though Freddie was a very tired bird, he could not resist coming out of his cage to see his visitor. I was excited to see Amy and Freddie meet at last. Amy took a selfie with Freddie, then interviewed me as her husband recorded us on video.

"I can sleep late tomorrow morning," I said to Amy.

She smiled. "Not so fast! Our morning show host wants to call you tomorrow morning at eight o'clock for a live radio interview!"

I stifled a yawn and turned to Freddie's cage. "Well, Freddie, I guess one more early morning won't bother us. At least we're home!"

There was one more thing to be done before Freddie and I could truly get some much-needed rest. I needed to be sure Freddie was okay physically after all he had been through. My friend Diane, who is knowledgeable about many kinds of birds, had stopped over. Freddie seemed to be fine, but just in case, she suggested that a friend of hers who is a wildlife veterinarian stop over to look at him.

Dr. Miller came late that afternoon to visually check Freddie and make a recommendation for treatment, if necessary. She thought Freddie looked okay and told me of things to look for that would indicate a problem. If necessary, she would recommend the appropriate avian (bird) veterinarian. "I find it hard to believe he was out there for ten days and looks as good as he does," Dr. Miller told us. She had a further comment: "Freddie is a very special bird." Gee, where have you heard that before?

In closing, I would like to tell you something that happened with Freddie a few months later. Fall had come, and there were fallen leaves everywhere. With leaf blower in hand, I went to the fence at the back of the yard. As I began the cleanup, I turned slightly toward the house. You would not believe what I saw. Freddie had opened the door enough to climb out onto the wooden railing just outside his room.

I shut off the leaf blower and calmly walked over to him. "Freddie, what are you doing out here?" I asked. Freddie continued to chew on the railing. I took hold of him and carried him back inside.

Afterward I examined the railing. The amount of wood he had chewed meant just one thing: Freddie had to have been there for plenty of time and could have taken off if he had wanted. Yet he never attempted to fly away. I guess that goes to show you that the old saying is true: there really is no place like home.

Westtown-East Goshen Regional Police Department
1041 Wilmington Pike West Chester, PA 19382
www.westtownpolice.org

Missing pet macaw "Freddie Mercury" found safe in Westtown Township

On Saturday, January 28 2017 at 4:18 PM members of the Westtown-East Goshen Regional Police Department responded to a home in the 500 block of West Pleasant Grove Road in Westtown Township, Chester County for an injured exotic bird in a tree on the property.

When Officers arrived on scene the property owner reported that the bird relocated from a tree to the roof of the home. Officers sought assistance from a local specialist in exotic animals who responded to assist. Police also received assistance from the West Chester Fire Department. Several attempts to rescue the bird failed and Officers on scene took photographs of the bird and these photographs were posted to the Westtown-East Goshen Police Association social media page seeking owner information.

A short time later police received a call from the Assistant News Director with WDEL News in Wilmington, Delaware and she related that the bird had been missing for nine days from the Wilmington area and attempts there to rescue the bird over the past week were not successful. WDEL Officials assisted Officers with making contact with the owner of the missing bird. The owner confirmed that the photos taken of the bird in Westtown was his missing macaw. The owner responded and worked with Officers to recover the bird and these attempts also failed. A plan was created for the owner to return before sunrise to retrieve "Freddie".

On Sunday, January 29 2017 at 8:00 AM Sergeant Wassell with the Westtown-East Goshen Regional Police Department returned to the 500 block of West Pleasant Grove Road to follow-up and contact was made with the owner of the bird along with the Thornbury Township residence that was originally contacted to assist police. Sergeant Wassell learned that the bird had just been recovered safely and that "Freddie" would be transported to a Vet to be checked.

The police department would like to thank everyone that called and responded to the social media post to connect the police department with the owner of the missing bird. This distance between the owner's residence in Wilmington and the location recovered in Westtown Township is 9.9 miles.

William Cahill
Detective/Lieutenant

Case: P17026762

If you would like to learn more about this amazing story, including video footage of Freddie fighting the hawk, a web browser search for the term "WDEL–Macaw" will provide links to all of Freddie's news items.

About the Author

Victor Rash was born in Dover, Delaware. He moved to Wilmington, Delaware, at a young age and has continued to reside there ever since. After serving four years in the US Air Force, he attended Brandywine College on a baseball scholarship. He has owned and been involved with training a standardbred racehorse that raced at the three racetracks in Delaware.

About the Book

This amazing true story will take you along on an emotional roller-coaster ride with Freddie Mercury, a four-year-old tropical parrot that flew off in the middle of the winter. See how an entire community, along with the help of a local radio station and an out-of-state police department, came together in an effort to rescue Freddie. He was fighting not only the cold but also birds of prey that had their sights set on him. It was a battle to survive each and every day, and Freddie was doing it all with little or no food or water.

Acknowledgments

As much as I enjoyed writing this book, it may never have happened if not for the help of several people.

The first mention goes to my friend April. If she had not told me about the bird rescue, I would never have met Freddie in the first place. During the time that Freddie was on the loose, April was tending to her father, who was extremely sick. She later told me that every night when she prayed for her father, she also prayed for Freddie's safe return.

Then there was Barbara Mitchell, the author of over twenty children's books. I had the pleasure of meeting her right around the time I was starting to write my book. I asked her if she would take a look at the first couple of chapters I had finished just to see if it was worthy of being published. She contacted me a short time later to let me know that she loved it. Barbara convinced me to keep going and helped me along as my reader, my editor, and my inspiration. Her encouragement helped to bring this book to completion.

Special thanks to Amy Cherry, assistant news director at WDEL Radio. From creating a special news segment, "The Freddie Watch," to summoning assistance from the Three Palms Zoo in lower Delaware, Amy was tireless in her determination to bring Freddie home. Her diligence brought this story to its ultimately happy ending.

To Ron of Ron's Tree Service. Ron selflessly used his own equipment while his amazing crew spent many hours trying to rescue Freddie from dangerous heights under difficult conditions.

Thanks to the Westtown–East Goshen Regional Police Department and the West Chester Fire Department for taking the call and helping to track Freddie's whereabouts.

Last, but certainly not least, is Diane K. I met Diane when Freddie was on the loose, and she was supportive in many ways. She has great expertise in working with tropical birds and has helped provide tips on how to care for Freddie. We have continued to be good friends.

I can't begin to count all the individuals from all over who followed Freddie's story and did whatever they could to help. I thank each and every one of you for your efforts and support in bringing my beloved Freddie home.

Printed in the United States
by Baker & Taylor Publisher Services